D1441967

Little Pebble™

MIGHTY MILITARY MACHINES

Fighter Planes

A 4D BOOK

by Matt Scheff

PEBBLE
a capstone imprint

Download the Capstone app!

- Ask an adult to download the Capstone 4D app.
- Scan the cover and stars inside the book for additional content.

When you scan a spread, you'll find fun extra stuff to go with this book! You can also find these things on the web at www.capstone4D.com using the password: fighterplanes.01129

Little Pebble is published by Pebble
1710 Roe Crest Drive, North Mankato, Minnesota 56003
www.mycapstone.com

Library of Congress Cataloging-in-Publication Data
Library of Congress Cataloging-in-Publication data is available from the Library of Congress website.

ISBN 978-1-9771-0112-9 (hardcover)
ISBN 978-1-9771-0118-1 (paperback)
ISBN 978-1-9771-0124-2 (eBook PDF)

Editorial Credits
Marissa Kirkman, editor; Heidi Thompson, designer;
Jo Miller, media researcher; Tori Abraham, production specialist

Photo Credits
Alamy: VDWI Aviation, 19; Shutterstock: Rick Parsons, 17; U.S. Air Force photo by Airman 1st Class Lauren Sprunk, 7, Airman Daniel Snider, 15, Senior Airman Kayla Newman, 13, Staff Sgt. Brian J. Valencia, 5, Staff Sgt. Clay Lancaster, cover' Staff Sgt. Natasha Stannard, 9; U.S. Air National Guard photo by Tech Sgt. Caycee Watson, 21; Wikimedia: U.S. Air Force photo by Chad Bellay, 11
Design Elements: Shutterstock: Zerbor

Printed and bound in China.
000309

Table of Contents

Fighter Planes

Look up!

It is a fighter plane.

In the Sky

These planes are fast.

They are strong.

They fly high.

They look for enemy planes.

They fire guns.

Boom! Blast!

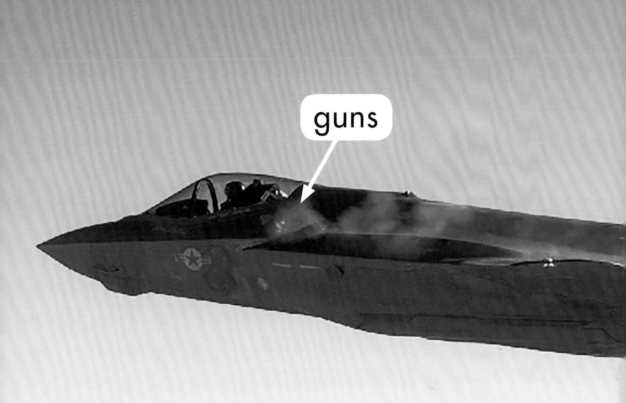

Parts

This is a jet engine.

It powers the plane.

The wings are long.

They lift the plane.

Up it goes!

wings

The pilot sits here.

The pilot flies the plane.

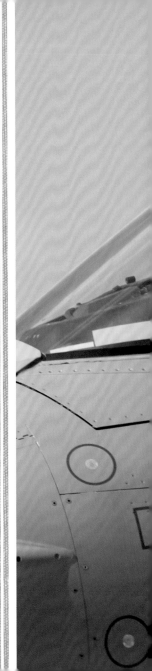

RESCUE

The pilot moves the stick.

It steers the plane.

Zoom! Woosh!

There goes a fighter plane.

Glossary

enemy—a person or group that wants to harm another person or group

jet engine—an engine that uses streams of hot gas to make power

pilot—the person who flies a jet or plane

steer—to move in a certain direction

wings—the parts of a plane that give it lift

Read More

Doeden, Matt. *The U.S. Air Force*. The U.S. Military Branches. North Mankato, Minn.: Capstone Press, 2018.

Parkes, Elle. *Hooray for Pilots!* Hooray for Community Helpers! Minneapolis: Lerner Publications, 2016.

Schuh, Mari. *Jet Planes*. Aircraft. North Mankato, Minn.: Capstone Press, 2013.

Internet Sites

Use FactHound to find Internet sites related to this book.

Visit *www.facthound.com*
Just type in 9781977101129 and go.

Check out projects, games and lots more at
www.capstonekids.com

Critical Thinking Questions

1. Who flies a fighter plane?

2. What does a fighter plane do while it flies in the sky?

3. Which part of the plane helps the pilot steer the plane?

Index